MW01672180

Original title:
Snuggle Bug's Nighttime Tales

Author: Miriam Kensington

ISBN HARDBACK: 978-9916-90-338-4
ISBN PAPERBACK: 978-9916-90-339-1

Fantasies in the Heart of the Dark

In shadows deep where secrets dwell,
Whispers rise like a distant knell.
Dreams take flight on fragile wings,
Cradled softly, the nightingale sings.

Stars shimmer down, a spectral glow,
Guiding hearts where the lost winds blow.
Each echo holds a tale untold,
In the silence, their voices bold.

Through tangled woods and starlit streams,
Reality dances with woven dreams.
Hope flickers in a candle's spark,
Lighting paths in the heart of the dark.

Embrace the magic, the unknown bliss,
For within the shadows, we find our wish.
A universe waits, vast and stark,
Fantasies live in the heart of the dark.

Cuddly Critters’ Chronicles

In the meadow soft and bright,
Bunny hops with pure delight.
Squirrels dance from tree to tree,
Nature’s joy for all to see.

Teddy bears with stitched-up dreams,
Whisper secrets, hear the beams.
Fluffy friends in playful chase,
Cuddly hugs in warm embrace.

Nighttime Nook of Wonders

Stars above begin to twinkle,
Moonlight casts a gentle sprinkle.
Crickets sing a lullaby,
As the day bids sweet goodbye.

Clouds drift slowly, dreams take flight,
In the calm of peaceful night.
Fireflies dance with glowing grace,
In this nook, our hearts find space.

Sagas in the Starlit Haven

Ancient tales told under skies,
Where the nightingale gladly flies.
Stories woven into the air,
Magic lingers everywhere.

Glistening stars whisper old lore,
Of adventures waiting at the door.
In this haven, dreams ignite,
Underneath the velvet night.

A Cradle of Cozy Moments

Blankets wrapped and pillows stacked,
In this warmth, our hearts unpacked.
Laughter echoes, stories shared,
In this cradle, love is spared.

Moments linger, time stands still,
Sharing whispers, sweetened thrill.
Cocoa sips and quiet sighs,
Underneath the starlit skies.

Whispers of Moonlight

In the night, shadows dance,
Whispers soft as a glance,
Moonlight drapes the earth's embrace,
Casting dreams in silver lace.

Stars above, a gentle choir,
Singing songs of sweet desire,
Each gleam tells a secret tale,
Floating soft on a nightfall gale.

Cozy Dreams Await

Beneath the quilt, warm and snug,
Nighttime's pull, a tender hug,
Eyes grow heavy, breathing slow,
Into dreamland, softly flow.

Gentle whispers, stories shared,
Comfort found, love declared,
In the silence, hearts unite,
Cozy dreams await tonight.

The Blanket of Stars

Stretched across the endless sky,
A blanket where the ancients lie,
Woven gems that softly gleam,
Encasing all in a cosmic dream.

Each twinkle holds a wish of yore,
Memories echo forevermore,
Underneath this radiant dome,
Stars whisper secrets of their home.

Tales of the Twilight

Twilight casts its gentle hue,
Painting skies in shades so blue,
Stories linger in the air,
Of fleeting moments, dreams laid bare.

As day bows down, night takes flight,
Shadows bloom in fading light,
In this magic, hearts will sway,
Finding peace at close of day.

Huddled in Nighttime Stories

In the quiet of the dark, we dwell,
Echoes of tales only we can tell.
With shadows dancing on the walls,
We find solace as adventure calls.

A flickering candle casts warm light,
In this embrace of the cozy night.
Each word woven, a magic thread,
Filling our hearts with dreams to spread.

The laughter lingers, the whispers fade,
As characters come to life, unafraid.
Every page turns with a gentle sigh,
Transporting us to where hopes fly high.

Huddled close, we lose all our fears,
The night becomes ours, adorned with cheers.
In stories shared, our spirits soar,
In the comfort of night, we long for more.

Wrapped in a World of Dreams

Nestled in clouds of soft delight,
Dreams take flight into the night.
Wrapped in warmth, a gentle embrace,
We drift through realms, a sacred space.

Each whisper carries a hidden vow,
In this world, we live somehow.
Stars above twinkle with glee,
Telling secrets, just for you and me.

With moonlight guiding our playful chase,
We wander freely, finding our place.
Imagination paints the skies,
In this sanctuary, reality flies.

Wrapped in dreams, our hearts ignite,
Chasing shadows into the light.
In slumber's arms, we come alive,
In this world of dreams, we truly thrive.

Comforting Silhouettes of Sleep

Silhouettes dance against soft hues,
Embracing warmth in evening's muse.
The world outside fades into gray,
Comforting peace at the end of day.

Gentle breaths in a lullaby's flow,
Soft whispers where no worries grow.
Wrapped in a quilt, old stories breathe,
In the realm of sleep, we weave and believe.

Shadows whisper secrets untold,
Stories shared, both new and old.
Each fading light brings tender grace,
In the sanctuary of a dreamer's space.

Comforting silhouettes, we find our way,
Through the veil where night holds sway.
In the stillness, our spirits mend,
As the embrace of sleep begins to fend.

Whispers of Moonlit Dreams

In the silver glow of the night,
Whispers drift, chasing the light.
Dreams painted on the darkened screen,
Where magic lingers, soft and serene.

The moon casts shadows, a silent guide,
In this realm where wishes abide.
Each twinkling star, a hope set free,
Whispers of dreams, just you and me.

Through the silence, secrets unfurl,
A tapestry woven in a sleepy whirl.
In moonlit whispers, we find our way,
To a place where fears cannot stay.

With every sigh, the night unfolds,
A canvas bright with untold golds.
In the arms of darkness, we dare to dream,
Whispers of freedom in every gleam.

The Warmth of a Furry Heart

In softest fur, a heart beats slow,
With gentle paws, love's warmth will grow.
Whispers of comfort in the night,
Together, we share the fading light.

Through every scratch, and every lick,
Furry friends know just the trick.
In their embrace, worries drift away,
In the hush of dusk, we stay and play.

Cuddly Nights and Starry Sky

Under the blanket, we snuggle tight,
With dreams adrift in the starry night.
Eyes like lanterns, shining so bright,
In cuddly warmth, everything feels right.

A cozy haven, wrapped in love's glow,
Every heartbeat, a gentle flow.
In the silence, joy takes flight,
Whispered secrets, until the light.

The Enchantment of Nestled Dreams

Clouds of visions, softly we glide,
In realms of slumber, side by side.
Whirling dances of laughter and cheer,
In dreams, we're free, without any fear.

Every wish, a star we chase,
In the woven quiet, we find our place.
Nestled close, like the moon and tide,
With dreams entwined, we take our ride.

Moonbeam Stories of Warmth

Beneath the silver, a tale unfolds,
In moonbeam whispers, soft and bold.
The night is young, with stories to tell,
In warmth of hearts, we cast our spell.

A flicker of light, a shadow of play,
Moments of magic, in every array.
With every glow, we share our art,
In moonbeam stories, love's beating heart.

A Blanket of Stardust Wishes

Under the night’s soft cover,
Dreams like fireflies glance,
Each twinkle a gentle sigh,
Hope wrapped in a dance.

Cradled by the moon's embrace,
Heartbeats hum a tune,
Wishes ride on golden beams,
Glowing bright as June.

In the stillness, secrets swell,
Whispers float like dew,
A blanket spun from stardust bright,
Each twinkle known to few.

Beneath the vast and velvet sky,
We toss our dreams alight,
Like snowflakes on a winter's breath,
A stardust wish takes flight.

Stories Under a Silken Sky

Underneath the silken sky,
Tales begin to weave,
Each star a spark of memory,
In the night we believe.

Whispers float on gentle winds,
Carried through the trees,
Echoes of forgotten nights,
Dancing with the breeze.

With every tale that's softly told,
New dreams start to form,
Painting pictures in the dark,
A heart forever warm.

So gather near, let stories flow,
Like rivers through the night,
Below the stars, we find the path,
To our own guiding light.

The Cradle of Whispering Stars

In the cradle of night’s cool arms,
Stars begin to sway,
Each shimmer holds a tale untold,
In their soft ballet.

A hush falls over sleeping lands,
As whispers greet the moon,
Crickets play their lullabies,
In nature’s gentle tune.

Nestled in the cosmic embrace,
Dreamers drift away,
With the stars as our companions,
Guiding hearts in play.

In this cosmic cradle, dear,
Let’s softly drift and soar,
To the rhythm of the stars’ sweet song,
Forever wanting more.

Nighttime Adventures in a Furry Den

In a den where shadows play,
Furry friends abound,
Underneath the moonlit glow,
Magic can be found.

With twitching tails and bright, wide eyes,
Adventures call us near,
Exploring dreams in leafy realms,
Where laughter disappears.

Together in our secret world,
We dash and race and roam,
Through the thickets, wild and free,
The night feels just like home.

So gather 'round, my furry kin,
Let's chase the stars tonight,
In our cozy, heartfelt den,
We'll weave our dreams in light.

Pillow Forts and Dreamy Ports

In the corner a fortress grows,
Soft and cozy, where imagination flows.
Blankets draped, a shield from the day,
Whispers of dreams, where we want to stay.

Shadows dance in the candlelight's glow,
Adventurers brave, with stories to sow.
A world of wonders, where echoes sing,
Pillow forts built, to which our hearts cling.

The Sleepy Serenade of Nightfall

The stars begin their gentle call,
A lullaby drifts through the hall.
Moonlight soft on the window pane,
Sings to the weary, easing their pain.

Night wraps the world in a tender embrace,
Sleepy eyes close at a slow, sweet pace.
Dreams scatter like leaves in the air,
In the stillness of night, without any care.

Moonbeams and Melodies of Joy

Moonbeams dance on the silver sea,
Notes of laughter float wild and free.
Under the stars, we twirl and sway,
Melodies whisper the night into play.

Dreams woven with threads of light,
In joyful rhythms, we take flight.
Each note a pathway to wander far,
Guiding our hearts beneath each star.

The Luminescent Path to Wonderland

A pathway glows with a silver sheen,
Leading us into realms unseen.
Through the thickets, where wild things roam,
To a place where our spirits feel at home.

Glistening flowers in colors bright,
Blooming softly in the calm of night.
Every step brings a joy anew,
On the luminescent path just for you.

Cradled by the Night’s Harmony

In the silence, stars align,
Moonlight dances, soft and fine.
Crickets sing, a lullaby,
Night's embrace as dreams float by.

Whispers thread through twilight air,
A gentle balm for those who dare.
Night unfolds its velvet shroud,
Comfort found beneath the cloud.

Heartbeats sync with shadows near,
In this realm devoid of fear.
Swaying branches, breezy song,
Here, in peace, is where we belong.

The Nest of Gentle Night Tales

Underneath the starlit sky,
Tales of wonder drift and fly.
Softly spoken, dreams ignite,
In our nest, we find the light.

With whispers wrapped in soft delight,
Stories bloom within the night.
Every flicker, every sigh,
Cradled close, our hearts comply.

Adventures painted in moon's glow,
Warm embraces set to flow.
Tucked in tight, with love we weave,
In this nest, we dare to believe.

Whispered Dreams and Warm Wraps

Whispered dreams on feathered wings,
Comfort deep that nighttime brings.
Wrapped in warmth, the world grows hushed,
In this moment, hearts are flushed.

Stars above like lanterns twink,
In the stillness, we can think.
Close your eyes, let fantasies soar,
In this peaceful realm, explore.

Through the dark, our spirits glide,
In the dreams, we choose to bide.
Every thought a tender song,
With warm wraps, we all belong.

Cozy Adventures in the Dark

Close your eyes, the night is new,
Cosy corners, just us two.
Softly cradled in the gloom,
Let our laughter fill the room.

Every shadow tells a tale,
Mysteries of the night unveil.
Through our whispers, we ignite,
Cozy dreams in the dark light.

Hand in hand, let's bravely roam,
In silent nights, we find our home.
Sleepy eyes, but hearts so bold,
Adventures waiting to unfold.

Fables of the Fuzzy Nest

In the branches high, they weave a tale,
Where gentle winds sing like a warm veil.
A gathering of dreams, soft and bright,
A Fuzzy Nest cradles the stars at night.

Whispers of laughter float on the breeze,
A safe little haven among the trees.
With every rustle, a secret is shared,
In the heart of the woods, love is declared.

Stories of friendship and hope take flight,
As dawn paints the sky with hues of light.
Through shadows they dance, so wild and free,
These fables of joy, where we long to be.

Nestled together, they gather near,
A tapestry woven of hope and cheer.
In the cozy embrace of the twilight glow,
The Fuzzy Nest whispers what we all know.

Tales Wrapped in Warmth

Beneath the quilt of twilight's embrace,
Lies a hearth aglow, a welcoming space.
With stories entwined like threads in the loom,
Each tale softly whispers, dispelling the gloom.

Hot cocoa glistens in mugs held so tight,
As laughter and love dance softly in flight.
We gather around, our hearts intertwined,
In tales wrapped in warmth, we find peace of mind.

Snowflakes drift gently, a magical sight,
While memories flicker like stars in the night.
Each moment we share, a treasure to keep,
In the comfort of kinship, we drift into sleep.

So raise up your glasses, toast to the night,
For in every story, there's love and light.
Together we'll weave a tapestry fine,
Of Tales Wrapped in Warmth, forever entwined.

Moonlit Adventures of the Heart

Under the silver glow where secrets are spun,
The moon whispers softly; the journey's begun.
Through shadows and echoes, our laughter ignites,
On Moonlit Adventures, where dreams take their flights.

Each step is a story, a dance through the night,
With fireflies winking, guiding our sight.
In a world wrapped in magic, our hearts intertwine,
Through whispers of branches and trails that align.

With the stars as our map, we wander with ease,
Collecting the moments, like petals from trees.
There's wonder in every turn that we make,
On these heart-bound adventures, we shimmer and shake.

So let's chase the dawn as we weave through the dark,
With the moon as our lantern, igniting a spark.
In the journey of love, we're never apart,
On these Moonlit Adventures of the Heart.

The Sigh of a Sleepy Hug

When twilight descends and the world turns slow,
A sleepy hug beckons, a warmth we all know.
In the quiet of night, where dreams softly drift,
The heart finds its solace, a gentle gift.

With eyes softly closed, the comfort begins,
Wrapped in affection, where stillness wins.
Each sigh is a whisper, a lullaby sweet,
Embraced by the moment, where time feels complete.

As shadows grow long and the stars start to gleam,
We float into slumber, carried by dreams.
In the hush of the night, let the worries take flight,
In the Sigh of a Sleepy Hug, everything's right.

So hold me close, where the world feels just fine,
In this cocoon of warmth, your heart next to mine.
As we drift through the silence, the night softly clings,
To the Sigh of a Sleepy Hug, where love softly sings.

Hibernation Haven of Lullabies

In the cozy nook, soft whispers sigh,
Blankets wrap dreams, as moments fly.
Gentle shadows dance on the wall,
Nature's lullabies cradle us all.

Silent snow drapes the earth with peace,
In this haven, all troubles cease.
Stars twinkle bright through the frosty night,
While we nestle close, drifting in light.

Each heartbeat echoes, a soothing song,
In this sanctuary where we belong.
Time holds its breath, a sweet embrace,
In hibernation’s warm, tender space.

Dreams take flight on a cloud of bliss,
Wrapped in calm, we find our kiss.
Morning will come, but for now we sigh,
In this haven where our spirits lie.

Night’s Gentle Caress

The moonlight spills across the land,
With silken threads, it softly strands.
Crickets sing their evening tune,
While stars peek out, like gems in the dune.

The cool breeze whispers secrets low,
In night's embrace, we let worries go.
Shadows play in the silver glow,
As time drifts by, sweet and slow.

Wrapped in peace, the world feels right,
As dreams emerge to take their flight.
Night's gentle caress cradles each heart,
In this magic realm, we won't part.

With each pulse of the quiet night,
We find solace in the moon's light.
Together we linger, hearts in sync,
In this tender moment, we rise, we sink.

Stories Spun from Moonlight

Beneath the stars, tales intertwine,
In moonlit beams, our hearts align.
Whispers echo, secrets softly told,
In the shimmering night, dreams unfold.

Images dance in the silver sky,
As reflections twinkle, our spirits fly.
Ancient stories from long ago,
Flow like rivers, gentle and slow.

Weaving laughter with threads of fate,
Moments captured, we celebrate.
Each flicker of light, a memory bright,
In the canvas of night, a wondrous sight.

Time stands still in this sacred space,
As we find warmth in each other's grace.
With every sigh, our hearts conspire,
In moonlit dreams, we find our fire.

A Journey Through Fluffy Clouds

Floating high on a soft, white plume,
Where worries drift and spirits bloom.
The sky unfolds like a painter's brush,
In this serene, whimsical hush.

Cotton candy dreams twirl in the breeze,
With every glance, our hearts find ease.
Above the world, we rise and soar,
In a playful dance, forevermore.

Each cloud a castle, each dream a gate,
In this ethereal landscape, we levitate.
Together we glide through the azure sea,
With laughter as fuel, we’re wild and free.

As the sun dips low, painting the skies,
We chase horizons, where freedom lies.
In this journey, we find our truth,
Among fluffy clouds, in eternal youth.

Fables on a Feather Bed

In the night where dreams softly tread,
Tales unfold, like threads of red.
Whispers weave through the gentle light,
Fables dance in the still of the night.

Under stars with a shimmering glow,
Each story blossoms, ready to flow.
Fluffy pillows, comfort bestowed,
A world of magic, where hearts erode.

With every shape that shadows cast,
Echoes of laughter, a gentle blast.
Sleep's embrace, a tender hold,
Whispers of wonder, a tale retold.

In this refuge, dreams take flight,
Fables linger, courageous and bright.
Softly cradled, let worries flee,
On a feather bed, we're wild and free.

Twilight Whispers and Hugs

In twilight’s glow, secrets hide,
Soft whispers linger, hearts open wide.
A gentle hug, warmth in the dark,
Moonlit moments leave their mark.

Stars twinkle in a velvet sky,
Dreamers gather, letting time fly.
Each word shared, a precious thread,
Binding souls, where love is fed.

Underneath the silver veil,
Whispers drift like a soft gale.
Together we find our truest song,
In twilight’s arms, we all belong.

As night falls, the world grows still,
Embracing magic, hearts to fill.
With every hug, we softly sway,
Twilight whispers guide our way.

Snuggled Up in Stories

With blankets wrapped, we find our place,
In the glow of stories, a warm embrace.
Adventures start, where pages turn,
In every tale, there's more to learn.

Monsters lurk and heroes rise,
In hidden worlds beneath the skies.
Fables rich with laughter and tears,
Binding us close through all our fears.

The fire crackles, shadows glide,
Snuggled close, we take the ride.
Magic flows through every line,
In whispered tales, our hearts entwine.

Through words and dreams, we roam afar,
In stories told, we find our star.
Snuggled up, let the journey start,
In every story, we share a part.

The Embrace of Radiant Dreams

In the cradle of night, dreams softly sing,
A chorus of hope, the heart takes wing.
Radiant visions, glowing and bright,
Envelop us in their warm light.

Floating on clouds of vibrant hue,
Every wish a whisper, alive and true.
Stars dance lightly in the velvet sky,
In the embrace of dreams, we learn to fly.

With every heartbeat, we chase the dawn,
In luminous realms, where fears are gone.
Beneath the moon's watch, gentle and kind,
The embrace of dreams, forever entwined.

So close your eyes, let the journey start,
Feel the magic awaken your heart.
In the night's embrace, together we scheme,
Exploring the wonders of radiant dreams.

The Cozy Embrace of Starlit Hours

Under the blanket of twinkling skies,
Whispers of dreams begin to arise.
Gentle breezes sing a soft tune,
As starlight dances beneath the moon.

The night wraps us in a silken quilt,
With every star, a wish is built.
Time slows down, just like a sigh,
In this warm space where shadows lie.

Memories linger in the cool air,
Moments captured with tender care.
The world fades, it's just us two,
Finding solace in this view.

Each heartbeat echoes a sacred prayer,
In the quiet night, love’s magic is rare.
Together we bask in the glow so bright,
In the cozy embrace of the starlit night.

Tales from Under the Covers

Beneath the sheets where dreams take flight,
Soft stories whisper through the night.
Each page a journey, a world unknown,
In the cocoon where love has grown.

With every turn, a new delight,
Imagined realms bask in moonlight.
Heroes and shadows, laughter and tears,
Adventures unraveling through all our years.

Hidden treasures lie in your gaze,
As we dive deeper into this maze.
Fables weave as we softly sigh,
Creating memories that will never die.

Embraced by warmth, our secrets shared,
In this small nook, we're never scared.
Together we drift, afloat on dreams,
Life's sweetest magic in moonlit beams.

Lullabies of a Sleepy World

In the hush of night, the world slows down,
Dreamy melodies wear a sleepy crown.
Crickets play as the stars keep watch,
While hearts unite in a gentle swatch.

Clouds float softly, like whispers of silk,
As we sip on dreams like warm, sweet milk.
Every shadow sings a lullaby,
Guiding us softly to the sky.

Twinkling lights spin tales of old,
While moonlight bathes the earth in gold.
Wrapped in the night's tender embrace,
We find our peace, our sacred space.

With each breath, the world's aglow,
The sleepy rhythm in ebb and flow.
Together we rest, beneath the stars,
Woven in dreams, no worries, no scars.

The Soft Glow of Midnight Stories

At midnight's door, where shadows play,
Stories emerge in a warm ballet.
Glimmers of light dance through the dark,
As whispers ignite the dimming spark.

Pages turn with a gentle sigh,
Adventures blossom, too sweet to die.
Between every word, a heartbeat glows,
A voyage awaits as the wonder flows.

Hushed secrets shared in the flicker light,
Create a tapestry of dreams that ignite.
In this haven, time stands still,
With every tale, there's warmth to fill.

Gather round, let stories unfold,
Each one a treasure, worth more than gold.
In the soft glow of magic's embrace,
We find our refuge, our sacred space.

Twilight’s Tales Unfurled

The sun dips low, the shadows play,
With whispers soft, they fade away.
Colors blend in a gentle swirl,
Stories bloom as night begins to unfurl.

Stars awaken, a cosmic dance,
Guiding dreams with a glance.
In twilight's grasp, the heartbeats sing,
Embracing the magic that night will bring.

The Land of Flickering Dreams

In a realm where wishes glide,
Moonlit pathways take us wide.
Flickering lights in emerald hue,
Leading us to adventures new.

The whispers of night weave a spell,
A sanctuary where hearts can dwell.
With every flicker, hopes ignite,
Painting visions in the quiet night.

Whimsical Wonders of the Night

Bubbles of laughter, floating high,
In a tapestry of starlit sky.
Creatures dance on silver streams,
In the realm of whimsical dreams.

All around, magic twirls and spins,
As the moonlight softly grins.
In the whispers, secrets bloom,
Under the night’s enchanting gloom.

Cuddled in Fantasy

Wrapped in comfort, dreams take flight,
In the cradle of the night.
Imagination leads the way,
To lands where hearts forever stay.

Embers glow like thoughts of gold,
In stories waiting to be told.
Cuddled close, the world grows strange,
In the folds of fantasy, we change.

Gentle Hugs from the Starlight

In the quiet of the night,
Stars whisper soft and bright,
Their twinkles wrap around,
In a cozy, glowing sound.

A breeze flutters by,
Carrying dreams to the sky,
Cradled in the night air,
A journey without a care.

Moonlight spills like milk,
Over fields, soft as silk,
Each ray a gentle hug,
Nurturing the world's snug mug.

In this peaceful embrace,
Time slows down its race,
With starlight’s warm, sweet kiss,
You find yourself in bliss.

Dreams in the Fuzzy Glow

Underneath a velvet sky,
Dreams dance and gently fly,
Wrapped in a fuzzy glow,
Softly whispering, they flow.

Clouds drift like cotton candy,
Colors bright and dandy,
Each thought a tender thread,
Stitched with love, gently spread.

Stars twinkle in the blue,
Creating magic anew,
Painted visions in the air,
Whispers of dreams everywhere.

Hold tight to these sweet sights,
Through the calm of warm nights,
In the stillness, we sigh,
As dreams take us up high.

The Magical Embrace of Night

As dusk falls, the world sleeps,
The moon's light softly creeps,
Awakening the stars,
A symphony from afar.

Each twinkle tells a tale,
Of dreams that gently sail,
Through the vast, endless deep,
In the night, secrets keep.

Magic lingers in the air,
With each heart finding care,
Wrapped in shadows, so light,
In the embrace of the night.

With every sigh, we drift,
In a peaceful, cosmic gift,
A journey filled with grace,
Finding solace in this space.

Comforting Tales through Soft Sighs

In the stillness of the eve,
Stories linger, never leave,
Each sigh carries a whim,
Lighting the path, soft and dim.

The heart knows every word,
In the hush, dreams are stirred,
Whispers from the past rise,
Nestled within soft sighs.

Shadows weave a tender song,
In this place, we belong,
As memories softly swirl,
Fading into night's pearl.

With each breath, tales unfold,
A comfort in the cold,
Wrapped in warmth, we abide,
Through soft sighs, side by side.

Soothing Shadows of Slumber

In the quiet of the night,
Shadows dance with soft light.
Whispers drift on gentle sighs,
As the world slowly lies.

Dreams take flight on silver streams,
Easing worries, nurturing dreams.
Wrapped in warmth of tender grace,
Finding peace in this embrace.

Stars blink softly, one by one,
A lullaby for everyone.
Carried on the breeze so light,
Hushed by the deepening night.

Soothing shadows gently weave,
A tapestry for hearts to leave.
In slumber’s arms, we softly fall,
To the soothing night's sweet call.

The Whispering Quilt

Beneath the stars, a quilt unfolds,
Whispers of stories yet untold.
Each patch holds a memory bright,
Warming hearts in the cool night.

Blue and gold in the moon's embrace,
Threads of dreams in every space.
Softly stitched with love and care,
The quilt wraps us in a rare air.

Gentle murmurs weave through seams,
Carried softly, like our dreams.
In its folds, we find our rest,
A woven hug, a cozy nest.

With every fold, a tale is spun,
In the darkness, we are one.
Together wrapped in this embrace,
The whispers linger in this place.

Twilight Tales with a Twist

As twilight falls, the stories sway,
In the dusk where shadows play.
Tales of sprightly sprites and gnomes,
In hidden glens, they find their homes.

The moon leans low, with glimmering eyes,
Catching secrets, silent cries.
With a twist, the tale begins,
In the darkness, magic spins.

Crickets sing their evening song,
As the night stretches long.
With every line, a twist awaits,
Mysteries dance behind the gates.

Through whispered woods and starlit paths,
Characters await, holding their laughs.
In twilight's hush, let stories bind,
A world of wonder, intertwined.

Embraced by the Night

The night wraps gently, soft and near,
In shadows deep, we feel no fear.
Stars, like lanterns, dot the dark,
Guiding dreams with their bright spark.

Crickets chirp, a rhythmic tune,
The moonlight dances, silvered boon.
In this embrace, we find our place,
Heartbeats slow, a tranquil pace.

The world fades, and silence reigns,
In whispered calm, we break our chains.
Held by night's eternal grace,
We close our eyes, find solace space.

Embraced by dark, we softly sway,
In dreams' sweet arms, we drift away.
The night a cloak, warm and tight,
Wrapping us in its tender light.

Adventures Beneath the Moon

We wander where the wild things play,
Underneath the silver light,
Whispers dance in soft array,
Lifting hearts toward the night.

A river flows with dreams untold,
Guiding us through lands so wide,
With each step, new tales unfold,
In the moonlit, starlit tide.

Ghostly figures, shadows tease,
Laughing softly in the breeze,
Every rustle hints at fate,
In this realm, it’s never late.

So we chase the fleeting gleam,
Toward horizons, wild and bright,
In adventures, we dare to dream,
Underneath the shimm'ring night.

The Soft Glow of Nightfall

As day retreats and shadows grow,
A blanket wraps the world in peace,
The stars appear, a gentle show,
In twilight's arms, all troubles cease.

The moon ascends with silver grace,
Painting dreams upon the ground,
In this serene and quiet place,
Only whispers of night are found.

Soft breezes carry tales of old,
From ancient woods and fields of lore,
In every sigh, a heart unfolds,
Embracing all that came before.

So let us bask in night's embrace,
And find our solace in the glow,
In the soft, enchanted space,
Where hidden wonders gently flow.

Stories Under the Pillow's Kiss

In dreams we weave our tales so bright,
Beneath the covers, snug and warm,
With every breath, we take to flight,
To lands where magic holds no harm.

The pillow whispers secrets sweet,
Of dragons fierce and seas of gold,
A world where every heart can meet,
Where brave arise and fears grow old.

Every star a tale to share,
Every moonbeam casts a spell,
In slumber's hand, we find our care,
A gentle place to dream and dwell.

So sleep beneath the starry sky,
Embrace the stories passing by,
For in those dreams, we'll truly fly,
Under the moon's watchful eye.

Fables from the Softest Shadows

In whispers shared by candlelight,
Fables spring from shadows deep,
Tales of courage, love, and fright,
In the quiet, secrets keep.

The softest shadows tell their tales,
Of lovers lost and battles fought,
With haunted paths and hidden trails,
Every story, a lesson taught.

Beneath the stars, the echoes play,
Of wisdom wrapped in mystery,
In every pause, we find our way,
To weave the threads of history.

So gather 'round as night unfolds,
Let every fable make you whole,
For in the moonlight, life beholds,
Fables that whisper to the soul.

The Sleepytime Sanctuary

In a room of quiet hues,
Soft pillows, dreams to choose.
Moonlight dances on the floor,
Whispers gentle at the door.

Lullabies of night do play,
Guiding stars along the way.
Blankets wrap a tender hint,
Of a world where spirits glint.

In this haven, peace unfurls,
As slumbering minds explore swirls.
Time surrenders, gently bends,
In the glow where dreaming blends.

Every sigh, a story spun,
Until the rise of morning sun.
Rest, dear heart, the night is yours,
In the sanctuary that restores.

Resplendent Reveries

Beneath a sky of velvet sheen,
Awaken dreams to colors keen.
Whispers drift on breezes light,
As stars aglow in velvet night.

Every thought, a tapestry,
Woven through reality.
Fleeting moments caught in time,
Chasing echoes, sweet and prime.

With every heartbeat, visions bloom,
In the silence, find the room.
Let imagination soar and sway,
In this dance of night and day.

Sunrise breaks with golden grace,
Awakening in a soft embrace.
Resplendent dreams, forever near,
In the heart, a cherished cheer.

Celestial Cuddles

Nestled close in cosmic glow,
Whispers wrap like winter snow.
Hearts in rhythm, softly thrum,
Wrapped in warmth, love's gentle hum.

Stars above, a twinkling tease,
As night-time drapes with tranquil ease.
Fingers intertwine like vines,
In this moment, bliss defines.

Galaxies may spin and sway,
Yet in your arms, I long to stay.
Celestial cuddles, safe and sound,
In this orbit, love is found.

Drifting off to dreamer's land,
With open heart and open hand.
Together we will find our way,
In the night, forever stay.

Tales of the Midnight Whisper

In the hush of midnight's call,
Ears attuned to secrets small.
Stories woven on the breeze,
Carried softly through the trees.

Echoes of a distant time,
Gentle rhythm, gentle rhyme.
With every breath, a tale it spins,
Where the heart of magic begins.

Shadows dance in moonlit glow,
As whispered words begin to flow.
Legends wrapped in silver light,
Guiding souls through the deep night.

Listen closely, hear the sighs,
In the silence, ancient ties.
Tales that shimmer, tales that wane,
In midnight whispers, love remains.

Secrets of the Slumbering Woods

In the hush of the twilight, whispers flow,
Beneath ancient boughs where the soft shadows grow.
Creatures of night weave through misty air,
Guardians of secrets, both tender and rare.

Moonlight dances on leaves with glee,
Nature's own rhythm, a sweet symphony.
Every rustle and sigh tells tales untold,
The magic of night is a treasure to hold.

Stars peek down from their velvet throne,
Illuminating paths where the wild things roam.
In the heart of the woods, dreams take their flight,
Cradled in mystery, wrapped in the night.

As the world drifts on in a silken embrace,
The slumbering woods weave a tapestry of grace.
Each heartbeat of nature, a lullaby sung,
A sanctuary found, where the soul feels young.

Hugging the Night Sky

Beneath the expanse where the stars softly gleam,
I stretch out my arms and embrace every dream.
The universe whispers secrets anew,
Painting my heart with each color and hue.

Clouds drift like ships on an ocean of night,
Illuminated by constellations so bright.
Every twinkle a promise, each shadow a sigh,
Together we dance, you and I, night sky.

The moon serenades with a silvery tune,
Wrapping the world in the arms of the moon.
In a blanket of starlight, we courageously fly,
Holding onto wishes that drift on the high.

So, let's wander through galaxies, hand in hand,
Exploring the wonders of this dreamlike land.
With the night as our guide, we will soar and glide,
In the embrace of the cosmos, forever we'll bide.

The Magic of Nighttime Stories

When shadows stretch long and the stars start to glow,
Whispers of magic begin to bestow.
In the quiet of night, tales weave and twine,
Bringing forth wonder, both yours and mine.

A dragon might soar through a castle of dreams,
While witches brew potions in silvery streams.
With goblins and fairies, adventures ignite,
In the world of stories, everything's bright.

Under the blanket, we journey afar,
Past mountains of candy and rivers of stars.
Each page turning gently, a flicker, a spark,
Together we travel through realms made of dark.

As the night deepens and adventures unfurl,
Fables embrace us, like a warm, loving swirl.
Let's cherish the moments, this magical art,
For nighttime stories steal away every heart.

Fables Under the Blanket

In the cocoon of night, we dream and we weave,
Fables and tales that our hearts can believe.
Under soft linens, adventures take flight,
Painting the darkness with strokes of pure light.

A brave little mouse in a land far away,
Found a treasure of cheese at the break of the day.
With courage and kindness, he shared with the flock,
In a world of fables, friendship's the rock.

An owl tells the stories of ages gone by,
Wisdom in feathers, beneath the night sky.
Each creature a character, each sound a delight,
In the embrace of our dreams, we relish the night.

So gather your tales, let imagination flow,
Fables under blankets, where hearts gently grow.
Together we'll cherish each magical turn,
In the glow of the moon, let our spirits discern.

Murmurs of the Sleepy Breeze

The whispering winds, soft and low,
Carry secrets that only they know.
Gentle caresses on tranquil skin,
A dance of dreams as the night begins.

Moonlight spills through the trees so tall,
Its silver glow a tender call.
Nature's lullaby sings us to rest,
In the arms of peace, we are truly blessed.

Stars twinkle softly above our heads,
While shadows sway in the quiet beds.
The night hums sweetly, a soothing tune,
Until the sun greets the sleepy moon.

In every rustle, a promise unfolds,
Of nights more gentle than tales of old.
So rest your heart, let the dreams arise,
In the murmurs where comfort lies.

Under the Cover of Magic

Beneath the velvet of the night sky,
Wishes and dreams begin to fly.
Each star a spark of hope and cheer,
Whispers of magic, drawing us near.

The moon casts shadows, playful and light,
As fairy tales live in the heart of night.
With a sprinkle of dreams, we softly drift,
Wrapped in the comfort of a nighttime gift.

Silken threads of dreams weave through the air,
A tapestry woven with love and care.
In this silent world, the heart takes flight,
Under the cover of the soft, sweet night.

So close your eyes, let the wonders rush,
Feel the magic in the gentle hush.
Tomorrow awaits with its bright, new glow,
But for now, let the dreams softly flow.

Bedtime Blessings and Dreams

In shadows deep, where silence weaves,
The comfort of night through soft dreams leaves.
Candles flicker, shadows play,
As bedtime blessings embrace the day.

A gentle kiss, a whisper low,
Wrapped in the warmth of evening's glow.
Hearts are light, cares drift away,
As dreams await in the soft decay.

Each star a guardian, shining bright,
Guiding our souls through the tender night.
With every breath, let worries cease,
In a world of dreams, we find our peace.

So snuggle close, let love abound,
In bedtime blessings, we are found.
With whispers sweet, drift off to sleep,
In the cradle of dreams, our spirits leap.

Where Comfort Meets the Stars

In the quiet corner of night's embrace,
We find soft solace, a sacred space.
Where comfort meets the stars so bright,
We weave our wishes into the night.

A blanket of shadows, warm and deep,
Cradling hearts as they gently sleep.
The sky is a canvas, painted with dreams,
As moonlight dances in silver streams.

Gently we float on clouds of care,
Lost in the magic of dreams we share.
Each twinkle a promise of joy untold,
In the warmth of the night, our spirits unfold.

So let the stars guide us from afar,
As we drift together beneath their spar.
In this hush of night, we find our way,
Where comfort stays until the break of day.

Cozy Corners of Imagination

In the quiet nook where dreams are spun,
Soft whispers dance until the day is done.
A chair of dreams in soft twilight glow,
Where tales of wonder and laughter flow.

The pages flutter like autumn leaves,
In a world where every heart believes.
Each story waiting with a gentle sigh,
To guide our spirits as we learn to fly.

With pillows plump and warm tea near,
Our cozy corners banish every fear.
Adventure waits with each turned page,
Igniting visions, setting hearts ablaze.

In this haven where imagination dwells,
Each moment stitched with magic spells.
So come and lose yourself, be free,
In the cozy corners of fantasy.

Starlit Storybook Adventures

Beneath a sky where the starry tales gleam,
Whispers of journeys awaken a dream.
The moon is a lantern, glowing so bright,
Guiding young hearts through the velvet night.

Magic unfolds in the rustling leaves,
As fairy tales weave what each heart believes.
Adventures await with the night's gentle breath,
In stories that dance beyond life and death.

With dragons soaring through the twinkling skies,
And brave little heroes who never say die.
Every chapter a treasure, a path to unfold,
In starlit realms where courage is bold.

Let us sail on a ship made of light,
Explore every corner till day meets night.
For in these stories, we'll find a way,
To live our adventures, come what may.

The Dreamweaver's Embrace

In the arms of night, where shadows play,
The dreamweaver whispers and guides our way.
Soft strands of hope weave through our sleep,
Cradling our wishes, the secrets we keep.

Each golden thread, a vision set free,
Encircling hearts like a warm decree.
With every sigh, a new dream ignites,
Painting our minds with vibrant delights.

As we drift between worlds, both far and near,
The dreamweaver beckons, inviting us here.
To dance on clouds, to laugh and to cry,
In the tender embrace where our spirits can fly.

So close your eyes and let go of the day,
In the dreamweaver's arms, come out and play.
For in this embrace, we shall find our grace,
As stories unfold in a boundless space.

Lullabies from the Hearth

In the glow of embers, soft murmurs sound,
Lullabies from the hearth, where love is found.
Crackling warmth wraps around like a quilt,
With every note, a loving heart is built.

The shadows sway in a playful dance,
As dreams take flight on a whispered chance.
Soothe the worries, let the world fade away,
In gentle melodies that forever stay.

With stars above and the moon in sight,
Each lullaby cradles the deep of the night.
A tender promise in every refrain,
To shield our souls from sorrow and pain.

So gather close by the fire's warm glow,
And let the lullabies whisper and flow.
For in these moments, we learn to trust,
In the warmth of love, a bond that's just.

Adventures in Dreamland's Nook

In the corner where shadows play,
Whispers of dreams invite the sway.
Clouds drift softly on silver beams,
Magic awakens in moonlit streams.

A castle of stars glimmers above,
Where wishes and secrets are wrapped in love.
Flying with fairies, I twirl and spin,
Lost in the joy of this world within.

The rivers of time softly flow,
Each ripple a tale that only we know.
Creatures of wonder, in laughter they dance,
In the heart of this nook, we take a chance.

So close your eyes, let the currents take,
A journey through realms where dreams awake.
Together we'll wander, forever we'll roam,
In Dreamland's Nook, we always find home.

Hushed Secrets of the Twilight

As the sun dips low, the sky ignites,
Day surrenders to velvet nights.
Stars emerge, shyly glowing,
Tales in the hush are gently flowing.

Breezes whisper through old trees,
Carrying secrets on the night's ease.
In shadows soft, the world feels new,
Cocooned in mystery, we drift in blue.

The moon's embrace sings lullabies,
Filling the air with heartfelt sighs.
Every glance, a story unfolds,
In twilight’s hush, the night boldly holds.

Just pause a moment, breathe it in,
The magic of dusk where dreams begin.
With every heartbeat, the night awakes,
In hushed secrets, the soul partakes.

Fables Woven in Warmth

In crackling fires, tales come alive,
Whispers of fables, where spirits thrive.
Characters dance in the glow of the flame,
Each story a spark, each heart a name.

The gentle hum of a nightingale,
Sings of adventures in winds that sail.
With each verse told, warmth fills the air,
A tapestry woven with love and care.

Old legends linger, their essence strong,
Binding us closely in the gentle song.
Under the stars, we share and dream,
In fables, we find a soothing theme.

With every glance into the night sky,
New stories form, as moments fly.
Together we laugh, together we share,
In the warmth of our tales, none can compare.

The Gentle Heartbeat of Nighttime

As dusk descends, the world sighs soft,
Crickets serenade from the treetops aloft.
In the hush between breaths, the real and the dream,
Nighttime unfolds, like a silver seam.

The moon, a guardian, watches above,
Casting a light like a promise of love.
In shadows that dance, secrets entwine,
Every heartbeat a story divine.

Stars wink playfully, a celestial choir,
Filling the night with a luminous fire.
In the embrace of the cool night air,
A gentle rhythm that whispers, “We care.”

So listen closely, to the night’s gentle heart,
With every pulse, we’re never apart.
In the stillness of hours, our dreams take flight,
In the heartbeat of nighttime, everything’s right.

Stories Cradled in Cloud

In whispers soft, the tales do rise,
Like fluffy clouds in painted skies.
They dance with dreams, they twist and weave,
A tapestry of hopes, believe.

Each story lingers, sweet and warm,
Through stormy nights, they keep us calm.
In every sigh, a world unfolds,
In silver threads, the heart beholds.

A lullaby that floats on air,
Each word a blessing, light as prayer.
They cradle us on gentle beams,
In cotton realms, we spin our dreams.

So close your eyes, let visions flow,
For in the clouds, our spirits glow.
With every story shared at dusk,
We find our light, our sacred trust.

Adventures in the Dreamscape

Through realms of night, we start to roam,
In dreamscapes vast, we find our home.
With wings of light, we take our flight,
Through sparkling stars, we chase the night.

Mountains high and valleys deep,
In whispered tales, the shadows leap.
Every corner holds a spark,
Guiding us through the endless dark.

With each adventure, new and bright,
We forge our fate with pure delight.
In starlit skies, our spirits dance,
Embracing every mystic chance.

So come, dear friend, let's journey far,
In dreamscapes wild, we find our star.
For in this realm, we stand as one,
In endless quests, we've just begun.

The Comfort of Cozy Curled

Nestled close where warmth abounds,
In secret corners, joy is found.
With tender hearts and soothing sighs,
We wrap ourselves in moonlit ties.

The world outside fades into hush,
As time slows down to let us brush.
Each cozy curl, a soft embrace,
In this warm nook, we find our place.

With blankets thick and stories shared,
In whispered tones, our dreams are bared.
Through every laugh and gentle tear,
We build a world that feels so near.

So let us linger, holding tight,
In cozy curls, we find the light.
For here, we weave our sweetest song,
A melody that will last long.

Secrets of the Soft Night

The soft night breathes its quiet tales,
Through velvet skies and starlit trails.
In shadows deep, the secrets lie,
Whispers of wishes let out a sigh.

Each twinkling star a tiny spark,
Guiding our hearts through the dark.
In moonlit dreams, we learn to see,
The beauty of all that’s meant to be.

With every rustle, the night reveals,
Hidden truths that the silence heals.
In gentle glow, our fears take flight,
As we embrace the warmth of night.

So listen close, as night unfolds,
In every secret, a story told.
With open hearts, we’ll find our way,
In the soft night’s gentle sway.

The Enchantment of the Sleepy Hollow

In the hush of twilight's glow,
Whispers dance where shadows flow.
Trees entwined in secrets old,
Stories waiting to be told.

Moonlight weaves a silver thread,
Guiding dreams where spirits tread.
Frogs croak softly by the stream,
In Sleepy Hollow, all is dream.

Crickets serenade the night,
Stars, like lanterns, burn so bright.
The wind carries tales anew,
Of goblins, fairies, and their crew.

Close your eyes, and you will find,
Magic lingers, softly wind.
In Sleepy Hollow, peace abounds,
Where the heart of night resounds.

The Dream Weaver's Secret

In a realm where dreams take flight,
A weaver spins through velvet night.
With silken strands of hope and fear,
She crafts the visions drawing near.

Golden threads of laughter weave,
Into pockets where we believe.
Whispers linger in the air,
Wrapped in magic, light as prayer.

Each pattern holds a story's grace,
A tapestry of every place.
The weaver smiles, her fingers dance,
Inviting all to take a chance.

So close your eyes, let visions bloom,
As dreams unveil life's hidden room.
Unlock the secrets, set them free,
In the weaver's world, you'll find the key.

Bedtime Tales Beneath the Stars

Gather 'round, the stories flow,
Beneath the stars, soft winds do blow.
Whispers carry through the night,
As dreams take shape in silver light.

Once there lived a brave young knight,
Who chased the shadows, spread the light.
With a heart so pure and strong,
He faced the dark where fears belong.

A wise old owl perched on a tree,
Told tales of love and bravery.
Each story glows like fireflies,
Guiding us through starry skies.

So snuggle close, let dreams begin,
In every tale, our hopes can win.
Beneath the vast and twinkling dome,
Bedtime calls us all back home.

The Warmth of Night's Embrace

The moon spills silver on the ground,
In night’s embrace, all is profound.
A gentle hush blankets the sky,
As stars awaken, shining high.

The world transforms, a tranquil place,
Where shadows dance in soft embrace.
With every breath, let worries cease,
In this stillness, find your peace.

Crickets chirp their lullaby,
As time flows gently, dreams draw nigh.
Wrapped in warmth, we softly sigh,
In the night, we learn to fly.

So close your eyes and drift away,
In night’s embrace, we choose to stay.
With every heartbeat, let love soar,
For in the night, we find what’s more.

Cuddle Companions

In the blanket's warm embrace,
We find our little space.
Soft whispers fill the room,
Dispersing all the gloom.

Eyes close and hearts align,
As we drift, we intertwine.
Dreams unfold on starry skies,
With every breath, love sighs.

Tangled limbs, a gentle dance,
In this moment, we take a chance.
Cuddle closer, don’t let go,
In the warmth, our spirits glow.

Together in this perfect night,
Cuddle companions feel so right.
With you here, I am whole,
Forever bound, heart and soul.

Enchanted Evening Echoes

Beneath the twilight's gentle veil,
We hear the whispers, soft and frail.
Moonlight dances on the ground,
In this magic, love is found.

Stars wink bright from way up high,
Sharing secrets in the sky.
Voices carry through the night,
Echoes sweet, a pure delight.

Shadows play and twirl around,
As we lose our hearts, unbound.
Every glance, a story told,
In the night, our dreams unfold.

Hand in hand, we stroll along,
In this moment, we belong.
The world fades, it's just us here,
In this evening, love is clear.

The Lullaby of Soft Shadows

Soft shadows dance upon the wall,
Whispering secrets, they softly call.
Wrapped in dreams, we find our way,
In the twilight's warm display.

Gentle sighs and tender light,
Guide us through the tranquil night.
Every moment feels so right,
In the arms of soft delight.

Crickets sing a lullaby sweet,
As the world fades, we find our beat.
In the hush, our hearts will sway,
Floating softly, come what may.

Close your eyes, let worries cease,
In this moment, find your peace.
Soft shadows cradle you and me,
In their arms, we'll always be.

Adventures in Sleepy Hollow

In Sleepy Hollow, shadows linger,
Whispers of adventure beckon, they finger.
Through meadows green and paths of gold,
Every story waiting to unfold.

With the moonlight as our guide,
Together, we take a thrilling ride.
Owls hoot softly in the trees,
As we chase the evening breeze.

Mysterious tales fill the air,
Of hidden treasures, a journey rare.
Hand in hand, we seek the light,
In this land of endless night.

Magic lingers in every glance,
In Sleepy Hollow, we take our chance.
With laughter ringing through the air,
Adventures bloom, a boundless affair.

Enchanted Encounters at Dusk

In twilight's glow, the world stands still,
Magic dances on the breeze,
Whispers woven with the night,
Stars awaken, hearts at ease.

Moonlight spills on hidden paths,
Where shadows play and secrets lie,
A fleeting touch, a knowing glance,
In enchanted realms, we fly.

The air is laced with fragrant blooms,
As laughter twirls like fireside tales,
Time slows down in this soft space,
Where love's sweet song prevails.

Embrace the dusk, let worries fade,
With every pulse, the magic grows,
In these moments, forever stays,
An enchanted dream that softly glows.

The Quilt of Cozy Dreams

Beneath the stars, we drift away,
In the warmth of a cotton seam,
Patchwork feelings layered tight,
Crafting colorful, cozy dreams.

Each square a memory, stitched with care,
Whispers of laughter, shared delight,
Faded stories, new ones bloom,
As we share this quilt tonight.

Threads of joy connect our hearts,
Woven with hopes and soft goodbyes,
In the gentle folds love resides,
A world created where warmth never dies.

Wrapped in comfort, we float away,
In the softness of this balm,
The night unfolds, our spirits play,
Embracing peace, enveloping calm.

Chasing Shadows and Sweet Whispers

In the twilight, shadows blend,
Soft whispers beckon, drawing near,
A dance of light and dark begun,
Echoes of laughter fill the sphere.

Through the trees, we chase the night,
Where secrets twirl in playful queues,
A tender sigh, a fleeting glance,
Under the sky dressed in deep blues.

The moon she smiles, our guiding light,
As dreams entwine beneath her glow,
Chasing shadows that stretch and fade,
In the magic, we learn to flow.

With every breath, the whispers grow,
Tales of wonder come alive,
In this realm where wishes spark,
We embrace the night, and thrive.

Fireside Tales of the Softly Snoozing

By the fireside, embers glow,
Tales of wonder gently weave,
Among the warmth, our dreams take flight,
As the world outside begins to leave.

Softly snoozing, the night unfolds,
With whispered tales that soothe the soul,
In these moments, time is lost,
As the stories begin to roll.

Crackling sparks tell of olden days,
Knights and dragons, love's bold quest,
Circling flames cradle our hearts,
In the warmth, we find our rest.

As yawns escape, we lose the light,
Wrapped in dreams, we softly sway,
Fireside tales keep fears at bay,
Together, we drift away.